SMITHSONIAN INSTITUTION

WAR BACKGROUND STUDIES

NUMBER THREE

THE PEOPLES *of the* SOVIET UNION

By

ALEŠ HRDLIČKA

(PUBLICATION 3690)

CITY OF WASHINGTON

PUBLISHED BY THE SMITHSONIAN INSTITUTION

JULY 15, 1942

The Lord Baltimore Press
BALTIMORE, MD., U. S. A.

THE PEOPLES OF THE SOVIET UNION [1]

By ALEŠ HRDLIČKA
Associate in Anthropology, Smithsonian Institution

In 1919 the first issue of this monograph was published by the Smithsonian Institution under the title "The Races of Russia." Since then the old Russia has passed on to a great new political unit known as the Union of Soviet Socialist Republics, or, briefly, as the Soviet Union.

The U.S.S.R., up to 1939, consisted of 11 voluntarily bound together republics which embraced all the territories of former Russia except the westernmost portions from Finland to Bessarabia, which had been severed from Russia after the first World War. These lands in a large measure again became part of the Soviet realm in 1939 and 1940, so that at the time of the German invasion, in June 1941, the Soviet Union consisted of 16 associated republics.

PRESENT POPULATION

The present population of the U.S.S.R., including the occupied regions, is generally estimated at close to 200,000,000. In January 1939, the date of the last Soviet census, with additions for the several units that joined the Union or were constituted later, it was as follows:

Republic	1939 Population
Great-Russia (S.F.S.R.)	109,278,614
Ukrainian	38,900,000
Bielorussian	10,300,000
Uzbek	6,282,446
Kazak	6,145,937
Georgian	3,542,289
Azerbaidjan	3,209,727
Moldavian	3,200,000
Lithuanian	2,880,000
Latvian	1,950,000
Tajik	1,485,091
Kirghiz	1,459,301
Armenian	1,281,599
Turkmenian	1,253,985
Estonian	1,120,000
Karelo-Finnish	463,100 [2]

[1] This paper is based on the writer's observations during three study trips to Russia and Siberia; on reliable historical records; and on official data of the Soviet Union. Thanks are due to the Soviet Embassy in Washington which has helped me with the latter. For a more detailed discussion of Russian history, the writer would recommend particularly the various articles on the subject in the Encyclopedia Britannica, especially the eleventh edition.

[2] Exclusive of inhabitants remaining in ceded Finnish area.

Between January 1939, the date of the census, and the end of June 1941, when the invasion took place, the population of each of the above units, except perhaps the last three, increased by about 1.9 percent, the total reaching close to or even over 197 million.

The percentage of natural yearly increase, compared with that of some other countries, is as follows: [3]

Russian Slavs	Soviet Union as a whole	U. S. A. (White)	England and Wales	Germany	Italy
1.5	1.4	0.8	0.25	0.8	0.9

Of the total 1939 population of the older 11 republics, 48 percent were males, 52 percent females; and there was an exceptionally high proportion of young people, over 45 percent being then under 19 years of age. The conditions have probably not changed materially since, up to the outbreak of the present war. In the summer of 1939, when the writer visited the Soviet country,[4] the preponderance of young people and of children was everywhere very noticeable.

The number of different peoples making up the Soviet Union is but little apparent until one enters the home regions of some of the groups in Asia, and even there, were it not for variation in garments, decoration, beard and hair dressing, and other secondary features, the differences would seldom be of a pronounced nature.

Taking the present Soviet population as a whole, it may be estimated to be roughly eight-tenths White, about one-tenth Yellowbrown, and the rest intermediate. There are no Blacks. Even what remains of the Yellowbrown stocks is rapidly being diluted by White admixture. As all the peoples in the Union have equal status guaranteed by the Constitution, as the physical, mental, and social differences among them are not great enough to lead to racial antagonism, and as the Russians have always been free mixers, regular intermarriages among the White and other groups are common, as well as propitious, and there is a natural steady progress toward a general blood union.

THE PEOPLING OF RUSSIA

Prehistory.—Up to the middle of the Quaternary period or Ice Age, the vast stretches of European as well as Asiatic Soviet Union were still devoid of human occupation. According to present-day evidence, it was only during the Mousterian or Neanderthal phase of man, and later, that

---

[3] Comparative data kindly furnished by L. E. Truesdell, Bureau of the Census, Department of Commerce.

[4] See "Anthropologist in Russia," Scientific Monthly March–June, 1942.

sparse human contingents began to spread over the more southern parts of these regions. At the end of the last glaciation or soon thereafter the early comers had reached the Crimea, other southern parts of European Russia, and as far at least as Uzbekistan, where recently (1938) the Leningrad anthropologist Okladnikov found in a cave, with Mousterian implements, the remains of a Neanderthal child. Farther east, along the upper Yenisei, Angara, and Lena Rivers and in the Lake Baikal region, occur the remains of later, upper paleolithic and highly interesting neolithic populations, the latter offering close resemblances to some of the American Indians. Upper paleolithic and especially neolithic men reached also over a large part of the European as well as the more southern Asiatic portions of the country.

Early and later historical data.—From the time of the neolithic men to the dawn of historical times, both the European and Asiatic parts of what is now the Soviet Union were extensively although sparsely peopled, and there began taking place in the more southern parts of the country in Europe and Siberia some large-scale displacements.

About 600 B. C., the European region of what was to become Russia comprised the area now occupied by Finland, Karelia, Estonia, Livonia, the higher Volga, and the main central regions, peopled sparsely by the "Finno-Ugrians," a somewhat Mongoloid stock speaking Finno-Ugrian (Uralo-Altaic) dialects, and connected with the original Hun Magyar, Turcic and other related elements of Asia. At the same time the region that is now southern Russia, aside from some older tribes such as the Cimmerians and Taurids, was occupied by partly nomadic (east), partly sedentary and agricultural (west) tribes known to the old Greeks collectively as "Scythians." The more eastern nomadic parts of this loose complex were doubtless Tatar, the sedentary western portions probably early Slavic. Lithuania, then occupying the territory that after the thirteenth century became Eastern Prussia, had an old and probably already mixed European population of its own, while Poland was always essentially Slav.

It was in these earliest historical times also that the Greeks established a number of trading posts and small colonies along the southern coasts of the territory, particularly in the Crimea, the names and remains of which exist in those parts to this day.

In the Arctic regions lived the Mongoloid forefathers of the Lapps, and farther east the Samoyeds.

In the Asiatic portion of the present Soviet Union, over the southern steppes, roamed the Tatars, Kirghiz, and related groups; while more to the south were the Turkmenian and related central Asiatic aggregations.

In Siberia, the neolithic population had passed apparently into the numerous paleo-Asiatic groups, and well before the beginning of the Christian era these were being pushed northward by the Mongol groups from farther south. This large movement of peoples, of which there are many evidences, resulted in many displacements, leading perhaps even to immigrations into the American continent.

As to earlier movements of peoples over what are now the European Soviet territories, many details are lost or obscure. Facilitated by the vast unobstructed grassy southern flats, many such movements occurred, some of much importance. These movements were from all directions except from the Arctic and the northeast, but particularly from the east westward, from the south northward, and eventually from the west eastward.

The "drives" from the east were those by more or less powerful groups of the Mongoloid nomads from the less hospitable Asiatic regions, where the climate was becoming drier. The invaders were the descendants of the old nomadic "Scythians," now known as the Hun, Bolgar, Magyar, Ugrian, Avar, Polovetz, Tatar, and Mongol, and their incursions plagued eastern and even central Europe from the fourth to the thirteenth centuries and even later. They overran generally parts of what is now Ukrainia, and some reached as far as Poland, eastern Germany, and Pannonia (a larger part of which became "Hun-land, Hungary"). The Huns under Attila penetrated in fact as far as northern France, where in 451 on the "champs de Chalôns," near the Marne, they suffered a fatal defeat.

The advances from the south were made by the Greeks, Venetians, Genoese, Khazars, and Turks; those from the northwest by the Goths, Varangians (Swedes), and Germans; and from the west by the Slavs, who eventually spread over wide areas, with later immigrations of varying magnitude of Jews, Germans, Poles, Czechs, and Rumanians. The more important of these processes deserve more detailed attention.

MOVEMENTS OF PEOPLES IN EUROPEAN RUSSIA

THE SCYTHIANS

The peoples of what are now the European parts of the Soviet Union first began to be better known as a result of the famous march into their country of Darius Hystaspes—the first "Napoleon"—about 512 B. C., and more especially through the writings of Herodotus, about 450 B. C. Of those populations that were mainly of Asiatic origin, by far the most prominent were the "Scythians," whose territory embraced practically the whole present southern Russia below about 50° N. latitude. Peoples of related origin covered the country from the Urals to Finland, and from the Volga to the Baltic. They were subdivided into numerous tribes and differed somewhat in blood, but all belonged to the Turkish, Tataric, Finno-Ugrian, and Laplandic subdivisions of the great Ural-Altaic stock of Asia. All these peoples, including the Scythians proper, had in common more or less marked Mongoloid features, many were nomadic or semi-nomadic, none originally being strictly agricultural, and except where they were in prolonged contact with other peoples, such as in the case of the Scythians with the Greeks, the Bolgars with the Khazars, or the Finns with the Scandinavians, their culture was of a primitive order.

The term "Scythians" deserves a few comments. Owing to their war-like qualities and the direct intercourse with them by the earlier Greeks, few "barbaric" nations of the pre-Christian era have been more discussed and few peoples since have given rise to more speculation as to their ethnic identity. On the basis of present historical and archeological knowledge it may safely be said that the early Greeks applied the term "Scythians" not to a race, but to a mass or conglomerate of peoples, partly nomadic and partly agricultural, who occupied the southern part of Russia when the Greeks began to explore and colonize the coasts of the Black Sea.[5] The main strains of the more eastern nomadic Scythians were undoubtedly Tatar and Turkish. To the west of the Borythenes (Dnieper); however, and particularly in present Volhynia, Bukovina, and Galicia, the principal and possibly exclusive element of the population from the earliest times was of European extraction, and this stock it seems could in the main have been no other than Slav. To it belonged tribes such as the "Neuri" (Nestor, the earliest Russian historian, mentions "Norici, who are the same with the Slavs"), the Alazones or Hali-zones (which in Russian would be Galitshani, from which Galicia received its name), and probably the Borysthenitae husbandmen.

The Scythians claimed to have roamed over or occupied for many centuries the country in which they were found by the Greeks. As shown by their customs described by the Greeks, and by the remains of their culture uncovered by archeological exploration, they were not wholly barbaric people; and contrary to what may be observed regarding later Tatar tribes, their warlike activities were directed mainly toward Persia and Asia Minor rather than toward Europe. It was to avenge their inva-sion of Medea and Persia that Darius undertook his memorable incursion into their country. Crossing the Hellespont into Thrace and proceeding then northward to and across the Danube, he reached as far as the "Oarus" River (supposed to have been the Volga, but more probably the Dnieper),

---

[5] Compare Ellis H. Minns, Scythians and Greeks. Cambridge, England, 1913.

only to find his great effort against the nomads quite futile. He finally barely escaped with the famished remnants of his army back across the Danube.

Scythia itself was subject to invasions, which require some consideration. Shortly after the commencement of the Christian Era, there are noted in Europe, and between Europe and Asia, movements of peoples which are commonly referred to as the "migrations of races," but which in the main were either incursions for conquest and plunder or the results of displacements, not seldom forcible, of tribal groups in regions where the density of population had surpassed the resources and the struggle for existence had become acute. They doubtless succeeded older movements of similar nature, of which there is no knowledge.

THE GOTHS

The first of the historic invasions into Scythia is that of the Goths, though some indications make it possible that this was preceded by less important offshoots from the same stock of people. The Goths were of Scandinavian origin, perhaps coming originally from or over the large island in the Baltic which still bears the name Gothland. From this they easily traversed the Baltic, known in the early Russian annals as the "sea of the Variags" or Scandinavians, and landed somewhere on what is now the Prussian coast, in the vicinity of the Vandals, a related group, probably not far from the mouth of the Vistula River. There they remained for a time; but when the number of their people increased, Filimer, their king, "decided that the army of the Goths with their families should move from that region," and "in search of suitable homes and pleasant places they came to the land of Scythia." (Jordanes, Getica, A. D. 551.) Whatever the details of their invasion, it is certain that by the beginning of the third century A. D. the Goths reached as far as the western parts of present Ukrainia and to the Black Sea and the Danube, as well as over the Carpathians. They then became known as the western and the eastern Goths, or Visigoths and Ostrogoths; and the latter, with whom alone we are here concerned, were found at the beginning of the fourth century ruling over the territory from the Carpathians to the Sea . of Azov. This rule they kept up until A. D. 375, when their state under Hermanric, together with the remainder of Scythia, was broken up by an overwhelming invasion of the Huns. Most of the Ostrogoths who survived sought refuge in the more southern parts of Europe; after Attila's death, or about 460, they moved bodily into Pannonia, granted to them by the Romans.

The Goth sovereignty in southwestern Russia was not an occupancy of a waste region by a new race. The territories in question were peopled, even though not densely, and remained so after the Goth domination; and their sedentary population was not Goth but in all probability Vendic or Slav, though there are also mentioned the Callipidae (Gepidae), the Alans, and the Heruli, who may have been some of Alpine and some of Nordic extraction.

The Goths were warlike northerners, who invaded Scythia in some force and brought with them their families. Owing to their favorable original geographical position and their sea activities, they were more advanced in general culture and especially in military art and equipment than the inland populations, who were being only slightly affected by the rest of the world. As a consequence of all this the northmen found no great difficulty in overrunning large areas occupied by the sedentary as well as the nomadic tribes, which had little political unity and no adequate powers of resistance. Some such tribes could even be employed against others, though of their own blood, and the invader finished by becoming the ruler. There are ample illustrations of similar processes elsewhere, such as many centuries later on the American continent, in Mexico and Peru. But the invaders, though they may create a state under their own banners, are seldom strong enough to give the conquered people their language, and though their name may remain, as happened later in Bulgaria and Rumania, the conquerors themselves disappear, either by being driven out or more commonly through amalgamation with the old population. Thus the Goths who gave way before the Huns were merely the usurping and then the ruling class, through their military organization; and when this power was overcome and they were driven westward, they left little behind them that would permanently affect the type of the indigenous populations. Moreover, they doubtless carried with them, in their families, households, and the army, many elements and perhaps even whole groups of the indigenous people.

THE HUNS

The great Hun invasion which overcame and drove out the Goths and which was one of the most sustained and serious of the Asiatic incursions of all times, obliterated Scythia and disorganized the whole region of the present Ukrainia and Bessarabia. The nomadic Scythians apparently receded to Asia; at all events they vanished completely as a power and entity. They left thousands of kourgans or burial mounds over southern Russia, though some such mounds may have been constructed also by other people.

The Hun swarm came from beyond the lower Don and Volga. In blood they were of Tatar or "Ugrian" derivation. Their language, like that of all the native population east of the Slav Russia, belonged to the Ural-Altaic. Contemporary accounts show them to have been typical Mongoloid nomads. From southern Russia they extended their incursions over most of western Europe. Soon after their defeat in France their dread chief Attila died, the power which they had established in Pannonia and central Europe rapidly crumbled, their confederates, among whom were some of the Germans and even Ostrogoths, broke away, and what remained of the horde, no longer able to hold its ground, retraced its steps eastward and was lost to sight. Exactly what effect this Hun invasion and occupation had on the population of southern Russia and central Europe is difficult to gauge, but it was probably mainly that of destruction or dispersion.

THE KHAZARS

What remained of the population in southern Russia-to-be after the Hun invasion now became gradually infiltrated with a new ethnic unit, the Khazars. The Khazars, according to many indications, were of Caucasian or anterior Asian extraction, and were related to the Georgians and Armenians. There were with them, however, also the so-called "black Khazars," who have not yet been identified. Their history in southeastern Russia extends over a considerable period of time—to the eleventh century. Between 600 and 950 the territory they controlled is said to have spread from the Caspian Sea to the Don and later even into the Crimea. They were relatively civilized people, who built small towns and engaged extensively in sea trade, which earned them the name of the "Phoenicians" of the Caspian and Black Seas. In the earlier part of the seventh century their power was such that they compelled the agricultural Slavs of the Dnieper and even those of the more northern regions to pay tribute. About 740 they accepted Judaism. But during the ninth and tenth centuries they were slowly outnumbered by the Russians, and in the eleventh century they practically disappear from the stage. Remnants of them probably still exist under different name or names in the Caucasus.

TURKISH AND TATAR TRIBES

The Khazar occupation of the regions which now form southeastern Russia was, however, far from uniform, dense, or continuously peaceful. The waves of incursion of the Turkish and the Tatar tribes from farther east followed at greater or shorter intervals, and over approximately the same roads—the broad open steppes traversed before by the Huns. Some of these invasions it is not necessary to enumerate in detail. The more important ones were those of the Bolgars in 482,[6] of the Avars in 557, and those of the Polovtsi (Kumans), Ugri (Magyars), Pechenegs, and related tribes, in the ninth and tenth centuries. Whatever the name under which they came, they were all of the Tatar or of Turkish extraction, with some admixtures. All were more or less nomadic and destructive, bent mostly on spoliation, but in the case of the major movements also on penetration toward the richer more central and southern parts of Europe, rather than on the conquest of Russia and the establishment there of a permanent new home; though some, such as the Polovtsi, Pechenegs, and others, became for a longer or shorter period settled in the territory. Taken collectively, these invasions resulted in a great retardation of the settlement of the southern parts of Russia. The hordes did not colonize or mix readily except through captives, and although remnants of them and mixtures were left, they made no very great impression on the sedentary population of the region.

THE SLAVS

Meanwhile, from as early as the times of Herodotus, the Greeks began to hear of tribes such as the Budini, which reached far eastward in the future Russia, and may have been Slav, for the root of the term is evidently Slavonic. Later on, in the fourth century, according to Jordanes,[7] the historian of the Goths, Hermanric conquered the Veneti, or Vends, which was the earlier generic name for the Slavs, the term "Slav" not appearing until after the close of the fifth century. In Jordanes' time, or about the middle of the sixth century A. D., the "populous race of the Veneti dwell near the left ridge of the Alps [Carpathians] which inclines toward the north, and, beginning at the source of the Vistula, occupy a great expanse of land. Though their names are now dispersed amid various clans and places, yet they are chiefly called Sclaveni and Anti. The abode of the Sclaveni extends from the city of Noviodunum and the lake called Mursianus to the Danaster, and northward along the Vistula. The Anti, who are the bravest of these peoples dwelling in the curve of the sea of Pontus, spread from the Danaster [Dniester] to the Danaper [Dnieper] rivers that are many days' journey apart." In another section of the work of the same author we read that these people

---

[6] These were the non-Slavic Bolgars from the Volga, who eventually left their name to the Slavonic state Bulgaria, south of the Danube.

[7] Mierow's version, Princeton, 1908.

"though off-shoots from one stock, have now three names, that is, Veneti, Anti, and Sclaveni." And "they now rage in war far and wide, in punishment for our [i.e. Goth] sins," though once "all were obedient to Hermanric's commands."

During the ninth and tenth centuries many Slav settlements or outposts are mentioned in Russia, by Arab traders mainly, as far north as the "Tchoud" country (Estonia), and as far west as the region between the Don and the Volga. Since the sixth and seventh centuries also there are historical data indicating extensive and in a large measure uninterrupted Slav population reaching from the Balkans to Pomerania, and from Bohemia and the Elbe over Poland, Galicia, what is now eastern Germany, and western Russia. This population is subdivided into numerous "families," tribes, or nations, which form as yet no great units. The term "Slavs" (from sláva, glory; slavit, to glorify), applied to these people, originated probably from their frequent usage in personal names of the terminal "slav," as in Jaroslav, glorifying the spring, Mstislav, extolling revenge, Boguslav, praising God, etc., which at that time was common to the whole people. Their earlier history and origin are lost in the mists of uncertainty, and their western contingents, except in language, were not clearly differentiated from the Germanic tribes. Tacitus evidently comprised all of them in his "Germania." They bore as yet none of the names by which they later became distinguished.

THE VARIAGS

The political unit of "Russia" did not come into existence until the ninth century. At that time according to the "Ancient Chronicle" of Nestor, the first Russian historian, there lived in the regions along and west of the Dnieper, and farther northward, the following Slav tribes: On the Ilman, the Novgorodci; on the upper Dnieper, Dvina, and Volga, the Krivitchi; between the Dvina and Pripet, the Dregovitchi; southeast of these, the Dierevliane (the woodsmen) ; from Teterev to Kiev, the Poliane (those of the flatlands) ; on the Bug, the Duliebi and Buzhane; on the Dniester and Bug, the Tivertsi and Ulitchi; in Volhynia, the Voliniane; on the Sozha, the Radimitchi; on the Oka, the Viatitchi; and on the Desna and Seim, the Severiane (the northerners).

These tribes, or local groups, were not yet united; and, according to Nestor, their dissensions finally led an influential elder to propose that they call some prince of foreign blood, of whom none would be jealous, and under whom, in consequence, it might be possible to merge all the subdivisions into one strong Slav state. The wisdom of this advice was acknowledged and the envoys called on certain princes of the Variags or Varangians, of Scandinavian origin. These were three brothers, the oldest of whom was named Rurik. They were offered the privilege of becoming the rulers of the tribes and, upon their acceptance, the Slav territories were divided among them; but the two younger brothers dying, perhaps not by natural means, shortly afterward, the entire nation became united under Rurik. However, in the opinion of some modern Russian historians the real facts were that the Slav and "Tchoud" tribes, suffering from repeated incursions of the much better armed and trained Scandinavians, hired other "Variags" for their protection, and these ended by usurping the ruling power over the tribes. Such was the birth of Russia. The term "Rus" appears at about the same time. It is in all probability derived from "rusij," fair-haired, blond, a general characteristic of the Slav people in these regions.

The Variags played a prolonged but steadily diminishing role in the Russian annals until they eventually disappeared, leaving little behind but some of their given names such as Oleg, Olga, etc., which to this day are in frequent use among the more northern Russians.

After Rurik the bulk of Russian history consists of internal accommodations, not seldom violent; of defensive or retaliatory external wars; of endless, fluctuating life-and-death struggles in the south and southeast with the Asiatic hordes; and of unceasing extension of the prolific Slav element in all directions where resistance was not insurmountable. This expansion took place toward the northeast and northwest, where gradually the Meria, Mordva, and other primitive Finnic strains were replaced or admixed and largely absorbed.

THE GREAT TATAR, OR "MONGOL" INVASION

Notwithstanding the many internal and external vicissitudes of the country, its elementary spread continued until 1226, when all southern Russia fell under the greatest blight that has yet afflicted it—the final and overwhelming Tatar or "Mongol" invasion. This invasion covered all present Ukrainia and beyond, and extended over much of Poland, Galicia, and Hungary, with some of eastern Germany. The southern Russians were overwhelmed and subjected to Tatar yoke, or forced to flee. The southern and southwestern parts of Russia became seriously depopulated and were occupied by the roaming Tatars of the "Golden Horde"; and Russia as a whole suffered from the effects of the invasion for 300 years. The invaders established themselves over the southeastern part of the country, and particularly in the Crimea, where they became a fixed element and developed a political unity of their own, which was ruled by their Khans until 1783, the year of their final submission to the Russians. To this day, however, a larger part of the highland population of the Crimea is more or less Tataric; and there is still in the central part of Moscow a section known as "Arbat," which used to harbor the visiting Tatars.

RUSSIAN CONQUEST OF SIBERIA

Long before this, however, the Russians spread over all the more northern regions of their present European domain, to and beyond the Urals, and even over Siberia. Expansion into the latter area deserves a few words of comment.

Up to the sixteenth century the vast region now known as Siberia was peopled exclusively by native peoples of paleo-Asiatic, Ural-Altaic, or Mongolian extraction. Most of them were more or less nomadic and in primitive states of culture. There was some but never any general political unity; and many of the groups whose forefathers had probably participated in the westward invasions had lapsed gradually into a numerically and otherwise weakened condition. It was such a state of affairs that awaited the ever-spreading Russian tide.

The first Russian traders crossed the Urals as early as the eleventh century, and perhaps even before; but such visits led to no consequences of importance. The conquest of Siberia took place in 1580. Yermak, a Don Cossack in disgrace, invaded the vast territory with 1,636 voluntary followers, and this handful of men practically secured the conquest of a territory considerably more than twice as large as the whole of Russia in Europe. Within 80 years after that the Russians had reached the Amur and the Pacific; and the rest, until the Soviet time, was merely a history of gradual dwindling of the natives and of Russian immigration.

MIGRATORY MOVEMENTS IN SOUTHERN RUSSIA

The cultural progress as well as the racial aspects of southern Russia were affected more by the great Tatar invasion of the thirteenth cntury than by any or perhaps all the previous ones. The descendants of the Tatars, together with other remnants, are found to this day in some numbers along the Volga and its southern tributaries, north of the Sea of Azov, in the Crimea and the Caucasus; while some Tatar blood can be traced in not a few of the southeastern Russian families. The effects of the resulting ethnographic changes are felt even now and have been utilized by the enemies of Russia against the interest of the country. This relates especially to Ukrainia (the "border province") or Little-Russia. No such subdivision existed before this last Tatar invasion, and the region of Kiev, now the capital of the Ukraine, was the old center and heart of all Russia. The Tatar massacres in part depopulated the region and created such terror that large numbers of the people fled westward into Galicia and Polish territory. There are differences of opinion as to how great the depopulation was, but that it was severe, though not complete, is indisputable. As all this is of particular importance at the present time it may be best to quote here from one of the foremost modern Russian historians who gave this question particular attention [8]:

The exodus from Kievan Rus took two different directions, and flowed in two different streams. Of these streams, one tended towards the West—towards the region of the Western Bug, the upper portions of the Dniester and Vistula, and the interior districts of Galicia and Poland . . . . This westward movement had a marked effect upon the fortunes of the two most outlying Russian provinces in that direction—namely, Galicia and Volhynia. Hitherto their position in the political hierarchy of Russian territories had always caused them to rank as lesser provinces, but now Galicia—one of the remote districts allotted only to *izgoi* princes of the house of Yaroslav—rose to be one of the strongest and most influential in all the southwestern region. The *"Slovo o Polku Igorově"* even speaks of the Galician Prince of its day (Yaroslav the Prudent) as "rolling back the gates of Kiev," while, with the end of the twelfth century, when Roman, son of Mstislav, had added the province to his own principality of Volhynia, the combined state waxed so great in population and importance that its princes became sufficiently rich and powerful to gather into their hands the direction of the whole southwestern region, and even of Kiev itself. In fact, the Ancient Chronicle goes so far as to describe Prince Roman as "the Autocrat of all the Russian land." Probably, also, this inrush of Russian refugees into Galicia and Poland explains the fact that annals of the thirteenth and fourteenth centuries frequently refer to Orthodox churches as then existing in the province of Cracow and other portions of the Southwest.

The same migratory movement may serve to throw light upon a phenomenon of great importance in Russian ethnography—namely, the formation of the Little Russian stock. The depopulation of Dnieprian Rus which began in the twelfth century was completed during the thirteenth by the Tartar invasions which took place between the years 1229 and 1240. For a long period after the latter date the provinces of ancient Rus, once so thickly peopled, remained in a state of desolation. A Catholic missionary named Plano Carpini, who traversed Kievan Rus in 1246, on his way from Poland to the Volga to preach the Gospel to the Tartars, has recorded in his memoirs that, although the road between Vladimir in Volhynia and Kiev was beset with perils, owing to the frequency with which the Lithuanians raided that region, he met with no obstacle at the hands of Russians—for the very good reason that few of them were left alive in the country after the raids and massacres of the Tartars. Throughout the whole of his journey across the ancient provinces of

[8] A history of Russia, by V. O. Kluchevsky, late professor of Russian history of the University of Moscow, 3 vols., vol. 1, pp. 194-196, London, 1911-13.

Kiev and Periaslavl, he saw countless bones and skulls lying by the wayside or scattered over the neighboring fields, while in Kiev itself—once a populous and spacious city—he counted only two hundred houses, each of which sheltered but a few sorry inmates. During the following two or three centuries Kiev underwent still further vicissitudes. Hardly had she recovered from the Tartar attacks delivered prior to the year 1240 when (in 1299) she was ravaged afresh by some of the scattered bands of Polovtsi, Pechenegs, Turks, and other barbarians who roamed her desolate frontiers. In that more or less grievous plight the southern provinces of Rus remained until well-nigh the middle of the fifteenth century. Meanwhile Southwestern Rus (now beginning to be called in documents of the period "Malaia Rossia" or "Little Russia") had been annexed to the combined state of Poland-Lithuania; so that of the Empire thus formed the region of the Middle Dnieper— i. e., old Kievan Rus—had now become the southeasternmost province or Ukraine. With the fifteenth century a new colonisation of the Middle Dnieper region began, to which two circumstances in particular contributed: namely, (1) the fact that the Steppes of the South were becoming less dangerous, owing to the dispersal of the Golden Horde and the rise of Muscovite Rus, and (2) the fact that the Polish Empire was beginning to abolish her old system of peasant tenure by quit-rent in favour of the barstchina system, which tended towards serfdom and therefore filled the oppressed rural population with a desire to escape from the masters' yoke to a region where they might live more freely. These two factors combined to set on foot an active reflex exodus from Galicia and the central provinces of Poland towards the southeasternmost borders of the Polish Empire—i. e., towards the region of the Dnieper and old Kievan Rus. The chief directors of this movement were the rich Polish magnates, who had acquired enormous estates in that part of the world, and now desired to people and reclaim them. The combined efforts of the immigrants soon succeeded in studding these seignorial domains with towns, villages, hamlets, and detached homesteads; with the result that we find Polish writers of the sixteenth century at once exclaiming at the surprisingly rapid movement of colonists towards the Dnieper, the Dniester, and the Eastern Bug, and lamenting the depopulation of the central provinces of Poland to which that movement had given rise. All things considered, there can be little doubt that the bulk of the settlers who took part in the recolonising of Southern Rus were of purely Russian origin—that, in fact, they were the descendants of those very Russians who had fled westwards from the Dnieper during the twelfth and thirteenth centuries, and who, though dwelling since among a Polish and Lithuanian population, had, throughout the two or three intervening centuries, retained intact their nationality.

The language of the new population of Ukrainia developed certain dialectical differences. In addition there arose in the course of time in the great territories over which the Russian people were spread some differences in the richness and nature of folk tales, folk poetry, dress, etc.—differences the perception of which by the Ukrainians has for a long time been assiduously fostered by the Germans on the basis of their cherished old "divide et impera" principle. Finally Ukrainia has received, together with Bessarabia, the mass of the Jewish immigration into Russia.

MALO-RUSSIANS, VELKO-RUSSIANS, AND BIELO-RUSSIANS

At about the same time that the terms Ukrainia or Mala-Rossia ("Smaller-Russia") came into vogue, there also began to appear those of Velka-Rossia ("Greater-Russia") and Biela-Rossia ("White Russia"), and those of Malorusi, Velkorusi, and Bielorusi, which are applied to their respective populations. These terms, like those of Ugro-Rusi, Rutheni, Gorali, etc., are partly conventional, partly environmental or geographical. The language and habits of the Bielorusi, who occupy the westernmost part of Russia north of Ukrainia, were gradually affected, though on the whole only moderately, by their relations with the Poles and Lithuanians; while those of the Velkorusi or "Moskvali" (Muscovites), who had spread over the central, northern, and eastern regions, were modified somewhat in turn by their associations with the Tchouds, Finns, and various other people of the Finno-Ugrian stock with whom they mingled and whom they freely absorbed.

Such were in brief the origin and nature of the three large subdivisions of the Russian people whom we meet today. The resulting differences between them, cultural, temperamental, and somatological, are not greater than those between some of the tribes of Germany or the people in different parts of England.

From the anthropological standpoint the Russians belong overwhelmingly to the great body of Slavs in general. Their cradle is the region extending from present Moldavia to the watershed of the upper Vistula. They doubtless descended from the old neolithic population of these territories, and were originally related to both the Alpine European stock and to what eventually became some of the Germanic tribes. But, like all large nationalities, the Russians in various localities show traces of admixture with the Nordic peoples on the one hand, and with the Finnish, Turkish, Tatar, Iranian, and other tribes on the other.

THE KAZAKS (COSSACKS)

A few words here are due to the famed Russian Kazaks, or as commonly misspelled in English, "Cossacks."

The term "Kazak" [9] is of Tatar derivation. It signified in Tatar an armed freebooter; in Kirghiz, a cavalryman; in Turkish, a light-armed mounted soldier. The term was applied by the Tatars to a variety of light cavalry before it became used by the Russians for similar troops formed along the southern boundaries of their country. They were settled

---

[9] "Kazakstan" is today used as the name of the Asiatic Tatar Soviet republic.

in various parts along these boundaries and became their privileged life-long and hereditary defenders. Owing to their prowess both as horsemen and fighters, the term "Kazak" in the course of time became surrounded, even in Russia itself, with a semiromantic and heroic halo, which was not wholly undeserved. The original Russian Kazaks of the fourteenth to sixteenth centuries were in the main of Ukrainian derivation; but in the course of time new contingents were formed progressively farther east, and these were of mixed Russian and Asiatic composition.

A few known details regarding the Ukrainian Kazaks may be of interest. During the fourteenth and fifteenth centuries Russian refugees before the invading Tatars are recorded to have settled on certain islands in the Dnieper River. They were hunters, fishermen, and, when occasion demanded, fighters, gradually developing into strong, bold, and resistant groups, loving the hard frontier life with its liberties and dangers. Similar groups developed in time all along the limits of the southern steppes, and became the scourge of the Tatars and Turks, though occasionally a source of trouble to the Poles and even the Russians. Their military value was in time recognized, leading to the regulation and extension of the Kazak system over southern Russia, Caucasus, central Asia, and Siberia, until the Kazak became the regular forerunner, scout, and protector of the Russian armies and Russian colonies from the Danube to the Pacific Ocean. Their faithfulness to the Czar was proverbial, and they were much used by the government for quelling internal troubles.

Until the first World War there existed about 12 subdivisions of the Kazaks, the best known of which were those of the Don, Orenburg, Ural, and Siberia. Their free institutions, interesting customs, and especially their exploits in the conquest of Siberia and in the Napoleonic invasion made their name famous. In the period following the 1917-1918 revolution the Don Kazaks, the chief unit, remained for a time on the side of the "interventionists," but since then have been strong components of the Soviet people. Their life is faithfully pictured in his "Quiet Flows the Don," by Shelekhov, himself a Kazak by origin and one of the foremost of present Russian writers.

THE WESTERN AND NORTHWESTERN NATIONS

THE POLES

The Poles, the old "Lekhi" and "Poliane," are Slavs, derived in pre-historic to early historic times, like the Russians, Czechs, and other peoples, from the common autochthonous Slav nucleus north and east of the Carpathians. They are admixed with the Russians and to some extent also with the Lithuanian, Nordic, and other elements. Notwithstanding their thousand years of agitated history, they are still a "young" people, full of innate strength, ability, and spirits, and as prolific as the Russians. Their unsettled history has been due to unfavorable boundaries and powerful neighbors, coupled with certain internal conditions.

THE LITHUANIANS

The Lithuanian territory lay originally along the Baltic, between the Visla (Vistula) and Dvina. At the time of their maximum political power their influence reached from the Gulf of Riga to Ukrainia. They extend at present from Poland and east Prussia to the borders of Latvia.

The Lithuanians are now a mixed group of people whose original racial identity is still a matter of controversy. Through their ancient "Baltic" tongue, which has many similarities with the Sanscrit and with the Slav, they are related to the latter. They have an admixture of all the elements surrounding them, the Poles in particular. Dialectically they were divided into three main branches, the Borussians (Prussians), the Latvis or Letts, and the Litvini or Lithuanians proper. The Borussians, whose home was in what is now eastern Prussia—the name of which, in fact, is derived from "Borussia"—were almost destroyed by the German "knights" in the thirteenth century, under the pretext of Christianization. In the words of one of the German writers himself (Schleicher, 1852): "Never has a pagan people, good, brave, and generous, been maltreated in a more cruel manner than the eastern Prussians. . . . . The history of their death struggle against the Teutonic order must be mentioned as one of the most sinister episodes of mankind." Some remnants of them still exist in the eastern part of East Prussia.

The Lithuanians, whose ethnographic limits are ill-defined, have had long political association, as well as some strife, with Poland; from 1721 to 1918 they have been connected with Russia, since 1940 with the Soviet Union.

THE LATVIANS

The Latvians, or Letts, are a mixed Baltic group related closely to the Lithuanians. From 1795 until near the end of the first World War, they were under Russia; in 1940 they became a part of the Soviet Union.

THE LIVONIANS

The true Livonians are almost extinct. Their country lay east and north of the Gulf of Riga, between that of the Letts and Estonia. From the early part of the eleventh century it was a bone of contention between the Russians, Germans, and Swedes, to fall in 1721 definitely to Russia. It is now occupied partly by Letts and partly by Estonians. The language of the Livonians belonged to the Finno-Ugrian family, and they were closely related to the Estonians.

THE ESTONIANS

The Tchouds or Estonians were originally a Finno-Ugrian tribe, occupying the larger part of the region of the old Livonia and present Estonia. Being weaker than their neighbors, from the eleventh century on they came alternately under the influence of the Russians, Danes, Germans, and Swedes, falling in 1710 definitely to the Russians. Estonia remained united with Russia until 1918, when it was severed from that country; in 1940 it united with the Soviet Union.

THE FINNS

The Finns represent the westernmost extension of the Finno-Ugrian stock. Although they have retained their language, their blood has become mixed with that of the Swedes, especially in the south. In fact, the inhabitants of the western and southern coasts are much more Swedish in type than Finnish; and there is also some Russian admixture. The more eastern related population, known as the Karelians, is better preserved.

The Finns, known also as Tchouds, or Chukhonians, reached their territory in protohistoric times. The first mention of the presence of Tchoud tribes along the eastern shores of the Baltic occurs in Tacitus, at the end of the first century A. D. Though always resisting domination by others, and for long periods of time more or less autonomous, they were in historic times never really free. From 1157, and probably earlier, their land was contended for and eventually taken over by the Swedes, to remain for several hundreds of years under their suzerainty. Soon after 1293, when Viborg was founded by the Swedes, their influence over the country began to be contested by the Russians, these conflicts culminating in the conquests of Peter the Great and finally those of Alexander I, which established the union of Finland as an autonomous grand-duchy with Russia. This union lasted until 1918, when Finland became an independent republic.

THE LAPPS AND SAMOYEDS

The most Mongol-like natives of European Russia, and undoubtedly of Asiatic origin, are the Lapps and Samoyeds. Their numbers are insignificant. They occupy the northernmost limits of the Finnish and Russian territories, the Lapps extending into Scandinavia. The present-day Lapps are much intermixed with the northern Whites.

FINNO-UGRIAN PEOPLES OF THE INTERIOR OF EUROPEAN RUSSIA

The Finno-Ugrians are located principally on the middle and upper Volga and the Kama, and represent the remnants of the primitive native populations that once covered much of central and eastern Russia. They have long been in the gradual process of amalgamation with the Russian population. They are known principally as the Mordva, Tcheremis, Voguls, and Votiaks.

EUROPEAN TURCO-TATARS

There are approximately seven million Turco-Tatars in European Russia and the Caucasus. They are divided into the Crimean Tatars, Kazan Tatars, the Bashkirs, the Tchuvash, and the Kirghiz, with many minor units. They still are scattered over a large portion of southeastern European Russia but are more or less admixed and have no racial cohesion.

PEOPLES OF THE CAUCASUS

The Caucasus has been since ancient times the eddy and refuge of remnants of nations, and there are in its fastnesses many interesting units, some of which it is difficult to classify. The strongest single element of the Caucasian population today, however, is the Slav (approximately 40 percent of the total), which is followed by the Turco-Tatar, Georgian, and Armenian.

THE ARMENIANS AND GEORGIANS

Both the Armenians and the Georgians are ancient White units. Both, though especially the Armenians, have suffered from many invasions, and both are mixed peoples.

The Armenians occupy also the adjacent parts of Turkey and Iran (Persia). They are known to history from at least seven centuries before Christ and are related primarily to the old Tadjik population of Iran, secondarily to the pre-Turkish peoples of anterior Asia. They are in general dark-complexioned people, of medium to moderately above medium stature and predominantly high brachycephaly. They are famed as traders. The part formerly under Russia joined the Soviet Union as one of its constituent republics after the 1917 Revolution.

The Georgians, or Gruzins, are an old and important trans-Caucasian group, related by language as well as by blood to a number of other tribes of the region. They appear in history in the twelfth century B. C. Their earliest name, curiously, was "Iberians," the same as that of the people of pre-Roman Spain, and some connection between the two, though not established, may have been possible. They were among the very earliest of Christians. Their capital, Tbilisi (520,000 inhabitants)—formerly Tiflis—dates from the middle of the first century A. D. At the beginning of the thirteenth century the country was devastated by Genghiz Khan, and this was repeated in the fourtheenth century by the followers of Timur. Toward the end of the eighteenth century it was largely under the domination of Iran and Turkey; in the period 1801 to 1829 it gradually joined Russia, in part voluntarily; and in 1921 it became a Soviet republic.

The Georgians or Gruzins proper constitute approximately 64.5 percent of the population of 3.5 millions. They are a highly brachycephalic people, which on one hand related them to the prevalent type among the Armenians, and on the other hand to the Tadjiks.

SPECIAL UNITS

THE JEWS

The Russian Jews are in the main the descendants of refugees forced out of Germany during the persecution of the race in the middle ages. Some Jews penetrated into Poland and Lithuania as early as the middle of the eleventh century, but by far the larger number came later, particularly under the Polish king, Kasimir the Great, whose wife was of Jewish extraction. From Poland they spread to Lithuania, Courland, and what is now Ukrainia and Bessarabia. Catherine II, particularly, opened to them the door of Russia.

A small branch of the Russian Jews differing in many respects from the remainder are known as the Karaites. They are principally agricultural and are settled in the Crimea, where they speak Tatar, and in western Russia, where they speak Polish.

The total number of Jews in European Russia before the first World War approximated 4,000,000, of which 1,300,000 were in Russian Poland, and 50,000 in the Caucasus. In addition there were about 50,000 in Siberia and central Asia.

Under the tsarist rule the Jewish poor were allowed to reside only in the towns and hamlets of the present Bielorussia and of the western part of Ukrainia, in the so-called "pale of settlement." Jewish children were admitted to secondary schools and universities only under a very limited percentage ratio.

In 1924 the Jewish poor from the hamlets began to settle on untenanted lands of the Ukraine, the steppe region of the Crimea, and in the northern Caucasus, Georgia, and Uzbekistan.

In 1928 the Soviets set aside the Birobijan district in the Far East as a settlement place for Jewish workers, and this has become the "Jewish Autonomous Region." It is one and a half times as large as Palestine. Since the beginning of the present war many Jewish refugees have been added to central Asia.

It is interesting to note that physically many of the Russian Jews of today resemble to a considerable extent the Russians themselves.[10] In Poland the approximation of the two types of population is much less apparent. The Karaites, whom some suppose to be the descendants of the Khazars, show anthropologically slight affinity with the Tatars.

THE GERMANS

The total number of Germans in the lands under Russian dominion amounted at the beginning of the first World War to a little over 1,800,000. They were scattered over all except the poorest parts of the empire, especially in the cities. In the Baltic provinces they were the landed proprietors. In southern Russia and other agriculturally rich regions there were German agricultural colonies, some recent, some of older formation. The main one of these was on the Volga.

The German influx into Russia started in the sixteenth century and was especially active during the reign of Catherine II. They came as artisans and merchants, frequently on invitation; and in 1762 they were invited to settle in parts of southern Russia in agricultural colonies, which gradually and in a scattered way extended to the Crimea, the Don, the Volga, and the Caucasus. These colonies received special privileges, were practically self-governing, and fused but little with the Russians. During the latter half of the nineteenth century German colonization in important parts of Russia, there are reasons to believe, was favored if not directed by the German Government for economic and perhaps strategic reasons.

The German nobles and landed proprietors in the Baltic provinces date in the main from the time of the attempts by the German Knights forcibly to "Christianize" the natives of the provinces and dominate the region.

After the establishment of the Soviets, the Volga Germans, who lived

---

[10] Compare Maurice Fishberg, The Jews. New York, 1911.

in a compact unit, were made into an Autonomous Volga German Republic. At the end of August 1941, as the invading Germans were forging eastward, the Volga group having become a point of danger to the state, the republic was abolished, the Germans were evacuated from the Volga region, and were resettled in parts of western Siberia and Soviet central Asia.

A study of the German relations with Russia shows that the latter has ever been a field for exploitation by Germany. Care was taken that the Germans in Russia should not disappear in the Russian mass and thus weaken Germany to the advantage of her neighbor, the dreaded sleeping Samson.

THE PRINCIPAL ASIATIC PEOPLES OF THE SOVIET UNION

The bulk of the people in Siberia and other Asiatic parts of the Soviet Union today are Russian. Among the rest, there are several groups that call for at least a brief special notice.

THE TAJIKS

Of the peoples of predominantly White but non-Russian origin, the principal ones are the Tadjiks, or as now regularly written Tajiks. This is an old brachycephalic Iranian stock, of slightly above medium stature, admixed somewhat with the Turkmen and differing physically as well as otherwise from both the Persians proper and from the Afghans. They live largely in a mountainous country and extend on the east into the Pamirs, on the south to Afghanistan. They constitute about three-quarters of the people of the Soviet Tajik republic.

THE TURKMEN

The Turkmen form the principal old central Asiatic stock. Where still better preserved they are distinguished by brachycephaly, above-medium stature, and characteristic facial features. They are to be counted with the Asiatic Whites, but in various regions there is much admixture with the Tatars. The Osmanli Turks of what is now Turkey were derived from this stock but became in turn much admixed with the peoples they conquered, both in Asia and the Balkans.

OTHER GROUPS

There is more or less of White admixture, some old, some more recent, in all the remaining Asiatic peoples of the Soviet Union, but the main

strains of these are the Mongoloid in the south and the related paleo-
Asiatic in the north. Among all the larger groups, especially in Azer-
baidjan, Uzbekistan, and the Tatar republics (Kazakstan and Kirghizstan),
there are individuals whom it would be hard to class as other than Whites,
but Mongoloid features, in various dilutions to purity, are predominant.
In the army, in the physical culture parades, and in the Pioneer groups,
where all dress alike, the differences are still further subdued and it
becomes difficult in cases even for an expert to be sure of what confronts
him. It is principally for this reason that there is no "race problem" in
the Soviet Union.

THE SMALLER SOVIET PEOPLES OF ASIA

Aside from the larger ethnic units in the south, there exist in the vast
stretches of Siberia, along the rivers, on the sea coasts, and in the forests,
many remnants of ancient tribes and peoples. In general these elements
are of paleo-Asiatic or Mongolian derivation, belong to various contingents of the Yellowbrown human complex, have more or less Mongoloid
features, yellowish to medium-brown skin, straight black hair; and individuals to whole groups among them show close resemblances to native
yellowbrown Americans. All these groups are already considerably admixed with Russian Whites, and these mixtures are gradually increasing,
so that within another century or two there will be left only a fusion.
Today, however, these groups still exist and have been known by various
names, most of which were nicknames or corruptions and have been
changed by the Soviet authorities. The principal names, past and present
are the following:

Old	New	Old	New
Abakan Turks	Khakasi	Negidaltsi	Elkenbeie
Aleuts	Unarigani	Orochi	Nani
Altaici	Oiroti	Oroki	Nani
Asiatic Eskimo	Iuits	Ostiaks	Khanty
Chukchi	Luoravetlani	Ostiaks-Samoyeds	Selkupi
Chuvantsi	Eteli	Ostiaks-Yenisei	Keti
Giliaks	Nivkhi	Samoyeds-Iuraks	Nientsi
Golds	Nanai	Samoyeds-Tavgiiski	Nganasani
Iukagirs	Oduli	Samoyeds-Yenesei	Entsi
Kamchadals	Itelmeni	Tungus	Evenki
Karagassi	Tophalari	Udiegeitse	Ude
Koriaks	Uimillani	Ulchi	Nani
Lamuts	Eveni	Voguls	Mansi
Lopars	Saami		

In addition there are in the north the Yakuts, speaking a Turcic language but decidedly Mongoloid in features; farther east the Chukchi, now

identified as physically the same as the Eskimo, and some of the Eskimo proper; in the southeast small contingents of the Koreans, Japanese, Chinese, and Mongols; in the southwest the Mongolian Kalmuks.

Before the German invasion in 1941, and to a greater extent since that event, the western regions of the Asiatic portion of the Soviet Union have received large accretions of workmen and refugees from Ukrainia and most other western parts of the country. Whole establishments with their staffs and workers have been transported there and reestablished. This is particularly true of the Urals, but also of Kazakstan, Uzbekistan, and other portions of Siberia and central Asia. These are permanent displacements that have already much altered the population as well as other aspects of these regions. The Urals are rapidly developing into the industrial as well as the population backbone of the Soviet Union, while the southern wastes and deserts are not only being restored through extensive irrigation and construction to what they were in the heyday of the ancient central Asian dominions, but have already advanced in population and otherwise beyond the old standards.

The population of the Asiatic portion of the Soviet Union is therefore now in a state of rapid change and great flux. Its heterogeneity is decreasing through intermarriages, and it is receiving a flood of new increments from European Russia. Paralleling the development of the western United States from the seventies onward, there is now going on a transformation of Siberia; a new human world is in formation there—a world of virile pioneers, farmers and workers, tinged slightly here and there by Mongoloid features, but essentially White, young and wholesome. This is the picture of Siberia as it is now unrolling before the observer.

LANGUAGES

There are spoken in the Soviet Union upward of 80 different languages, not to count those of various small groups; but the main medium of communication is the Great-Russian. Schooling is given in all the tongues, with the addition of the Russian; and they all have some literature of their own. They may be informally classed as European (Slavic, Lithuanian, etc.), Caucasic (many fragments), Southeastern-Asiatic (Semitic, etc.), Semi-Asiatic (or Finno-Ugrian: Finns, Karelians, Estonians, Volga groups), Uralo-Altaic proper (Tatar, Kirghiz, etc.), Turcic (Turkmenians, Yakuts, etc.), and Paleo-Asiatic (remnants of various aboriginal Siberian tribes). A thoroughly scientific classification would not only require much more space, but would also involve numerous difficulties, as the knowledge of some of the small-group languages is still imperfect.

PRESENT NUMBERS

It will be well now to give the statistics of the different main peoples here dealt with. The best data on this subject are those of the Soviet Census of January 1939. Excluding the numerous small contingents of Caucasus and Siberia, the figures are as given below. To bring them to date (except for the Baltic regions), they should be increased by approximately 1.4 percent for each year; from the total, however, there would have to be deducted the present war losses and those due to German massacres.

National composition of the population of the U.S.S.R. according to the 1939 census

(Not including Western Ukraine and Western Bielorussia)

	Nationalities	Number	Percentage of total
1.	Russians (Great-Russians)	99,019,929	58.41
2.	Ukrainians (Lesser-Russians)	28,070,404	16.56
3.	Bielorussians (White-Russians)	5,267,431	3.11
4.	Uzbeks	4,844,021	2.86
5.	Tatars	4,300,336	2.54
6.	Kazaks	3.098,764	1.83
7.	Jews	3,020,141	1.78
8.	Azerbaidjanians	2,274,805	1.34
9.	Georgians	2,248,566	1.33
10.	Armenians	2,151,884	1.27
11.	Mordvians	1,451,429	0.86
12.	Němtsi (Germans)	1,423,534	0.84
13.	Chuvash	1,367,930	0.81
14.	Tajiks	1,228,964	0.72
15.	Kirghiz	884,306	0.52
16.	Peoples of Daghestan	857,371	0.50
17.	Bashkir	842,925	0.50
18.	Turkmenians	811,769	0.48
19.	Poles [a]	626,905	0.37
20.	Udmurts	605,673	0.36
21.	Mariitsi	481,262	0.28
22.	Komi	408,724	0.24
23.	Chechentsi	407,690	0.24
24.	Osetians	354,547	0.21
25.	Greeks	285,896	0.17
26.	Moldavians	260,023	0.15
27.	Karelians	252,559	0.15
28.	Karakalpaks	185,775	0.11

National composition of the population of the U.S.S.R. according to the
1939 census—Continued

(Not including Western Ukraine and Western Bielorussia)

Nationalities	Number	Percentage of total
29. Koreans	180,412	0.11
30. Kabardinians	164,016	0.10
31. Finns [a]	143,074	0.08
32. Estonians [a]	142,465	0.08
33. Kalmuks	134,327	0.08
34. Latvians and Latgols [a]	126,900	0.07
35. Bolgars	113,479	0.07
36. Ingush	92,074	0.05
37. Adygeitsi	87,973	0.05
38. Karachaievtsi	75,737	0.04
39. Abkhasians	58,969	0.03
40. Khakasi	52,062	0.03
41. Oirots	47,717	0.03
42. Kurds	45,866	0.03
43. Balkartsi	42,665	0.03
44. Iranians	39,037	0.02
45. Lithuanians [a]	32,342	0.02
46. Chinese	29,620	0.02
47. Czechs and Slovaks	26,919	0.02
48. Arabs	21,793	0.01
49. Assyrians	20,207	0.01
50. Native Siberians and other small groups	807,279	0.48
Total	169,519,127	100.00

[a] At large.

PHYSICAL STANDARDS

Up to 1923 the peoples of the Soviet Union presented interesting demographic and consequent biological conditions. Hygiene and medical care were insufficient, in places almost wanting. The rivers for the most part were not yet harnessed, irrigation was but poorly developed, and communications were inadequate, with the result that serious droughts were followed by widespread famines. At the same time the birth rate was very high, reaching in some parts the yearly rate of over 50 per thousand, or more than twice that in other large European countries. The conditions outlined above also resulted in a very high death rate, particularly among the weaker elements of the population, both children and adults. Only the stronger and more resistant could survive under such disadvantages, but those who did survive constituted a stronger people of a higher biological value. It was thus that they were able to survive the first World War, the revolution, the interventionist and civil wars that followed, and the great famine that developed during these years; and it was thus that they still found strength to drive out all invaders, form a great state, stage since 1923 a striking development in many directions, and eventually stand and stem the attack of the greatest and most destructive military machine of all times.

Anthropologically, the peoples of the Soviet Union, in common with all other larger human contingents of modern times, are more or less admixed, and they present many grades and variants in stature, head form, and all other features. Of the large groups perhaps the most homogeneous are the Great-Russians. Except where mixed somewhat with the old Finno-Ugrians, they might justifiably be called a subrace of the White human stem. Their characteristics are well marked and include, on the average, light hair, bluish or gray eyes; rounded head; medium-featured face, pleasing and strong but not often handsome; well-proportioned to sturdy body, generally rather short but strong hands and feet. Their stature is not so high, blondness so pronounced, or eyes so often blue as in the Scandinavians, but their lightness is more general than with the Germans. The nose is never over-prominent, beaked, or very narrow, the lips are normally never thin, the jaws are strong, the teeth generally regular and in much better condition than in western Europeans or Americans. The beard, where still worn—which is now rare even among the older men—is as a rule more or less grizzly and ample in size.

The Bielorussians are in all these respects much like the Great-Russians, but there are some differences among the Ukrainians. The latter show less lightness of hair and eyes; there are more plump women among them, and more, even in the country, that are really beautiful in youth. More or less mixture with the Tatars or other non-Russian elements has taken place in the southern districts. In these regions too the people are predominantly of medium stature and brachycephalic, but in their features they resemble more the Slavs of Moravia and the Balkans.

The peoples of the Baltic republics, from Livonia northward, show occasional traces of the original Mongoloid Finno-Ugrian stock, but all through these parts both Nordic and Slavic features may commonly be encountered.

In Russian Galicia, Moldavia, and Bessarabia, the basic elements of the population are Slavs, kin mainly with the Ukrainians—most of them in fact are Ukrainians, and the type is similar. But there were also here, up to the 1941 invasion, numerous Jews, with some Poles, Bolgars,

Rumanians (many of whom themselves were originally Slavs, and preserve the same type), Gypsies, and other small contingents, which produced more or less physical diversity.

In the Crimea, which contains a mosaic of small ethnic groups with a predominance in the hills of the Tatars and their mixtures, there is no prevalent local type. The Tatars, or what remains of them, show Mongoloid features.

The Caucasus, a mountain complex over 900 miles long and 140 miles broad, with its many native groups of White people, appears to be less of a puzzle physically. There are two main types, that of many of the mountaineers proper, and that of the people of Trans-Caucasian Georgia and especially Armenia. But many detailed differences occur, not all of which are as yet capable of precise evaluation.

The native Asiatic groups, as already mentioned, show predominantly Mongoloid features.

CONCLUDING REMARKS

Leaving aside all details and localized ethnic peculiarities, we find that the racial problems of European as well as of Asiatic Russia, are relatively fairly simple. The situation may be summarized as follows: 1. There exists over portions of the European Russian territory a thin substratum of Finno-Ugrians, who carry varying but now diluted proportions of Mongoloid characters. 2. The southern portions of Russia from remote times have constituted a broad avenue for the movement of Asiatic peoples in a westerly direction. These peoples were partly of Iranian, but mainly of Turko-Tatar derivation, and most of the Turko-Tatars are mixed and intermediate peoples, partly White and partly Mongolian. Their influence, both racial and cultural, on southern Russia persists in a measure to the present day. 3. Along the Baltic there are remnants of Finnish tribes in the north and Letts and Lithuanians, of mixed composition, farther southward and westward. 4. All the rest of the great region of European Russia is Slav—Polish, and Bielo-Russian in the west, Velko-Russian or Malo-Russian (Ukrainian) in the center, south, and eastward.

European Russia is thus essentially a Slav country, and this is equally true today of Siberia and in large measure also of Soviet central Asia and the Caucasus. In southern Siberia and Soviet central Asia, however, there are still fairly large contingents of Turcic and Tataric derivation, while farther north are numerous remnants of paleo-Asiatic and Mongoloid origin.

From the anthropological standpoint, the Russian stock is well developed, virile, resistant, and full of potential force. It may truly be said to be a great human reserve of the European population. If up to recent times Russia had not advanced in culture as much as the western European nations, the causes, it can readily be seen, have been not inherent or racial, but geographic and circumstantial. Russia from its inception formed the buffer between the rest of Europe and Asia, as well as the principal check on the Turk, and it lacked largely the strong cultural stimuli that acted on the more western nations. That there was no inherent inferiority has been amply proved by the great progress of the country within the last score of years.

What will be Russia's future? The Russian Slavs, taken collectively, number today over 140 millions, and they are increasing yearly, by the excess of births over deaths, by approximately 1.5 percent. This rate of increase is greater than that of any other people in Europe except some of the Balkan branches of Slavs, and with the mass of the people belonging to the rural and worker population, cannot be expected to become much reduced in the near future. Such a rate of increase of this strong and able stock means a growing biological momentum. This insures that Russia must in future be expected to exercise important world influence, both anthropological and general.